FREE LOOPS

After working in Back or Front Loops Only on a row or round, there will be a ridge of unused loops. These are called the free loops. Later, when instructed to work in the free loops of the same row or round, work in these loops *(Fig. 3a)*.

When instructed to work in free loops of a chain, work in loop indicated by arrow *(Fig. 3b)*.

Fig. 3a   **Fig. 3b**

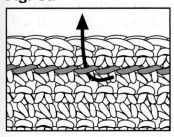 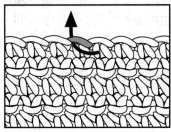

WORKING IN SPACE BEFORE A STITCH

When instructed to work in space **before** a stitch or in spaces **between** stitches, insert hook in space indicated by arrow *(Fig. 4)*.

Fig. 4

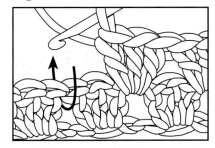

BACK STITCH

Come up at 1, go down at 2, then come up at 3 and go down at 4 *(Fig. 5)*.

Fig. 5

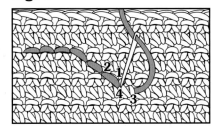

We have made every effort to ensure that these instructions are accurate and complete. We cannot, however, be responsible for human error, typographical mistakes, or variations in individual work.

Production Team: Writer - Sue Galucki; Technical Editor - Linda Luder; Artist - Lora Puls; and Photo Stylist - Sondra Daniel.

Booties made and instructions tested by Mike Cates, Katie Galucki, Donna Soellner, and Clare Stringer.

1. ALL ST~~~~

Finished Size: 0-3 m

MATERIALS
  Bedspread Weight Cotton Thread (size 10).
    Black - 65 yards
    White - 65 yards
    Red - 10 yards
  Steel crochet hook, size 7 (1.65 mm) **or** size needed
    for gauge
  Tapestry needle

GAUGE: 18 dc = 2"

Gauge Swatch: 1³/₄"w x 3³/₄"h
Work same as Sole.

STITCH GUIDE

> **DECREASE**
> Pull up a loop in next 2 sc, YO and draw through all 3 loops on hook **(counts as one sc)**.

SOLE

With White, ch 22.

Rnd 1 (Right side): 7 Dc in fourth ch from hook **(3 skipped chs count as first dc)**, dc in each ch across to last ch, 8 dc in last ch; working in free loops of beginning ch *(Fig. 3b)*, dc in next 17 chs; join with slip st to first dc: 50 dc.

Note: Loop a short piece of thread around any stitch to mark Rnd 1 as **right** side.

Rnd 2: Ch 3 **(counts as first dc, now and throughout)**, dc in same st, 2 dc in each of next 7 dc, dc in next 17 dc, 2 dc in each of next 8 dc, dc in each dc around; join with slip st to first dc: 66 dc.

Rnd 3: Ch 3, dc in same st and in next dc, 2 dc in next dc, (dc in next dc, 2 dc in next dc) 6 times, dc in next 18 dc, 2 dc in next dc, (dc in next dc, 2 dc in next dc) 7 times, dc in each dc around; join with slip st to first dc: 82 dc.

Rnd 4: Ch 1, sc in same st and in each dc around; join with slip st to first sc, finish off.

TOP

With Black, ch 52.

Row 1 (Right side): Sc in second ch from hook and in each ch across: 51 sc.

Note: Mark Row 1 as **right** side.

Rows 2-4: Ch 1, turn; sc in each sc across.

Rows 5-9: Ch 1, turn; decrease, sc in each sc across to last 2 sc, decrease; at end of Row 9, do **not** finish off: 41 sc.

Continued on page 3.

2

Row 10: Ch 1, turn; sc in each sc across.

Row 11: Ch 1, turn; decrease, sc in each sc across to last 2 sc, decrease: 39 sc.

Rows 12-14: Repeat Rows 10 and 11 once, then repeat Row 10 once **more**: 37 sc.

Edging: Ch 1, turn; sc in first 36 sc, 3 sc in last sc, sc in end of next 14 rows; working in free loops of beginning ch, 3 sc in first ch, sc in next 49 chs, 2 sc in next ch, place marker around last sc made for st placement, sc in same ch and in end of next 14 rows, 2 sc in same st as first sc; join with slip st to first sc, finish off: 124 sc.

Trim: With **right** side facing, join Red with slip st in marked sc; slip st in each sc across to center sc of last 3-sc group; finish off.

TONGUE
With Black, ch 12.

Row 1: Sc in second ch from hook and in each ch across: 11 sc.

Row 2 (Right side)**:** Ch 1, turn; 2 sc in first sc, sc in each sc across to last sc, 2 sc in last sc: 13 sc.

Note: Mark Row 2 as **right** side.

Rows 3-14: Ch 1, turn; sc in each sc across.

Rows 15-17: Ch 1, turn; 2 sc in first sc, sc in each sc across to last sc, 2 sc in last sc: 19 sc.

Rows 18 and 19: Ch 1, turn; sc in each sc across.

Edging: Ch 1, turn; sc in first sc, place marker around last sc made for st placement, sc in each sc across to last sc, 3 sc in last sc; working in end of rows, skip first row, sc in next 2 rows, 2 sc in next row, sc in last 15 rows; working in free loops of beginning ch, sc in ch at base of first sc and in next 10 chs; working in end of rows, sc in first 15 rows, 2 sc in next row, sc in next 2 rows, skip last row, 2 sc in same st as first sc; join with slip st to first sc, finish off: 72 sc.

TOE
Foundation Row: With **right** side of Tongue facing, join White with slip st in marked sc; ch 1, sc in same st and in next 18 sc: 19 sc.

Row 1: Turn; slip st in first 10 sc, place marker around last slip st made for st placement, ch 3, skip next 2 sc, slip st in next sc; **turn**; 7 dc in marked st, skip next 2 sts on Foundation Row, slip st in next st: 7 dc.

Row 2: Ch 3, skip next 2 sts on Foundation Row, slip st in next st, turn; 2 dc in first dc and in each of next 6 dc, skip next 2 sc on Foundation Row, slip st in next sc: 14 dc.

Row 3: Ch 2, skip next sc on Foundation Row, slip st in next sc, turn; (2 dc in next dc, dc in next dc) 7 times, skip next st on Foundation Row, slip st in next st: 21 dc.

Row 4: Ch 1, turn; sc in each dc across, slip st in last sc on Foundation Row.

Row 5: Ch 1, turn; sc in each sc across, slip st in last st on Foundation Row; do **not** finish off.

JOINING
Rnd 1 (Right side)**:** Ch 1, do **not** turn; sc in end of Foundation Row and in next 3 sc on Tongue, with **right** side facing, insert hook in same st on Top as last slip st of Trim **and** in next sc on Tongue, YO and pull up a loop, YO and draw through both loops on hook to complete sc, sc in next 51 sc on Top, insert hook in same st on Top as first slip st of Trim **and** in fourth sc from end of Tongue, YO and pull up a loop, YO and draw through both loops on hook to complete sc, sc in last 3 sc on Tongue and in end of Foundation Row on Toe, sc in next 21 sc; join with slip st to first sc: 82 sc.

Rnd 2: Ch 1, turn; sc in same st and in each sc around; join with slip st to first sc, finish off.

Rnd 3: With **right** side facing, join Red with slip st in same st as joining; ch 1, sc in same st and in each sc around; join with slip st to first sc, finish off.

Rnd 4: With **right** side facing, join White with slip st in first sc; ch 1, sc in same st and in each sc around; join with slip st to first sc, do **not** finish off.

Rnd 5: Ch 1; with **wrong** sides of Rnd 4 and Sole together, matching sts and working through **both** loops of **both** pieces, sc in same st and in each st around; join with slip st to first sc, finish off.

CIRCLES (Make 2)
With White, ch 4; join with slip st to form a ring.

Rnd 1: Ch 1, 6 sc in ring; join with slip st to first sc.

Rnd 2: Ch 1, 2 sc in same st and in each sc around; join with slip st to first sc: 12 sc.

Rnd 3: Ch 1, 2 sc in same st, sc in next sc, (2 sc in next sc, sc in next sc) around; join with slip st to first sc, finish off leaving a long end for sewing: 18 sc.

SHOELACE
With White, chain an 18" length; finish off.

FINISHING
Thread tapestry needle with one strand of White. Using photo as a guide for placement, back stitch 3 eyelets on each side of Top *(Fig. 5, page 2)*.

Thread tapestry needle with Shoelace and weave Shoelace through eyelets on each side of Top.

2. PLAIN JANES

Finished Size: 0-3 months

MATERIALS
Bedspread Weight Cotton Thread (size 10): 95 yards
Steel crochet hook, size 7 (1.65 mm) **or** size needed
    for gauge
Sewing needle and thread
5/16" Buttons - 2

GAUGE: 18 dc = 2"

Gauge Swatch: 1 7/8"w x 3 3/4"h
Work same as Sole.

SOLE
Ch 20.

Rnd 1 (Right side): Sc in second ch from hook and in each ch across to last ch, 3 sc in last ch; working in free loops of beginning ch *(Fig. 3b, page 2)*, sc in next 17 chs, 2 sc in next ch; join with slip st to first sc: 40 sc.

Note: Loop a short piece of thread around any stitch to mark Rnd 1 as **right** side.

Rnd 2: Ch 1, sc in same st and in next 17 sc, 2 sc in each of next 3 sc, sc in next 17 sc, 2 sc in each of next 2 sc, sc in same st as first sc; join with slip st to first sc: 46 sc.

Rnd 3: Ch 1, sc in same st and in next 17 sc, 2 sc in next sc, (sc in next sc, 2 sc in next sc) twice, sc in next 18 sc, 2 sc in next sc, (sc in next sc, 2 sc in next sc) twice; join with slip st to first sc: 52 sc.

Rnd 4: Ch 1, sc in same st and in next 17 sc, 2 sc in next sc, (sc in next 2 sc, 2 sc in next sc) twice, sc in next 19 sc, 2 sc in next sc, (sc in next 2 sc, 2 sc in next sc) twice, sc in last sc; join with slip st to first sc: 58 sc.

Rnd 5: Ch 1, sc in same st and in next 17 sc, 2 sc in next sc, (sc in next 3 sc, 2 sc in next sc) twice, sc in next 20 sc, 2 sc in next sc, (sc in next 3 sc, 2 sc in next sc) twice, sc in last 2 sc; join with slip st to first sc: 64 sc.

Rnd 6: Ch 1, sc in same st and in next 17 sc, 2 sc in next sc, (sc in next 4 sc, 2 sc in next sc) twice, sc in next 21 sc, 2 sc in next sc, (sc in next 4 sc, 2 sc in next sc) twice, sc in last 3 sc; join with slip st to first sc: 70 sc.

Rnd 7: Ch 1, sc in same st and in next 17 sc, 2 sc in next sc, (sc in next 5 sc, 2 sc in next sc) twice, sc in next 22 sc, 2 sc in next sc, (sc in next 5 sc, 2 sc in next sc) twice, sc in last 4 sc; join with slip st to first sc: 76 sc.

Rnd 8: Ch 1, sc in same st and in next 17 sc, 2 sc in next sc, (sc in next 6 sc, 2 sc in next sc) twice, sc in next 23 sc, 2 sc in next sc, (sc in next 6 sc, 2 sc in next sc) twice, sc in last 5 sc; join with slip st to Back Loop Only of first sc *(Fig. 1, page 1)*, do **not** finish off: 82 sc.

SIDES
Rnd 1: Ch 1, sc in Back Loop Only of same st and each sc around; join with slip st to **both** loops of first sc.

Rnds 2-5: Ch 1, sc in both loops of same st and each sc around; join with slip st to first sc.

Rnd 6: Ch 1, sc in same st and in next 21 sc, (skip next sc, dc in next sc) 8 times, skip next sc, sc in each sc around; join with slip st to first sc: 73 sts.

Rnd 7: Ch 1, sc in same st and in next 19 sc, skip next sc, dc in next 10 sts, skip next sc, sc in each sc around; join with slip st to first sc: 71 sts.

Rnd 8: Ch 1, sc in same st and in next 18 sc, skip next sc, (sc in next dc, skip next dc) twice, sc in next 2 dc, (skip next dc, sc in next dc) twice, sc in each sc around; join with slip st to first sc: 66 sc.

Rnd 9: Ch 1, sc same st and in next 17 sc, skip next sc, (sc in next sc, skip next sc) 4 times, sc in next 14 sc, place marker around last sc made for Strap placement, sc in each sc around; join with slip st to first sc, finish off: 61 sc.

STRAP
RIGHT BOOTIE
Row 1: With **right** side facing, join thread with slip st in marked sc; ch 1, sc in same st and in next 31 sc, leave remaining 29 sc unworked: 32 sc.

Row 2: Ch 18, turn; sc in second ch from hook and in each ch across, sc in next 32 sc: 49 sc.

Edging: Ch 1, turn; sc in each sc across to end of Strap, ch 4 (buttonhole); working in free loops of ch, sc in ch at base of first sc and in each ch across, (slip st, ch 2, hdc) in first unworked sc on Rnd 9 of Sides, [skip next 2 sc, (slip st, ch 2, hdc) in next sc] 4 times, [skip next sc, (slip st, ch 2, hdc) in next sc] twice, [skip next 2 sc, (slip st, ch 2, hdc) in next sc] 4 times, (slip st, ch 2, hdc) in first sc of Edging, skip next 2 sc, [(slip st, ch 2, hdc) in next sc, skip next 2 sc] 9 times, slip st in next sc; finish off.

LEFT BOOTIE
Row 1: Ch 17; with **right** side facing, sc in marked sc and in next 31 sc, leave remaining 29 sc unworked: 32 sc.

Row 2: Ch 1, turn; sc in each sc and in each ch across: 49 sc.

Row 3: Ch 1, turn; sc in first 19 sc, place marker in last sc worked, sc in each sc across; finish off.

Edging: With **right** side facing, join thread with slip st in marked sc; ch 2, hdc in same st, [skip next 2 sc, (slip st, ch 2, hdc) in next sc] 10 times, (slip st, ch 2, hdc) in first unworked sc on Rnd 9 of Sides, [skip next 2 sc, (slip st, ch 2, hdc) in next sc] 4 times, skip next sc, (slip st, ch 2, hdc) in next sc, skip next sc, [(slip st, ch 2, hdc) in next sc, skip next 2 sc] 4 times, slip st in next sc; working in free loops of ch, sc in each ch across, ch 4 (buttonhole), slip st in first sc on Row 3; finish off.

Sew button to Bootie.

3. LET IT SNOW

Finished Size: 0-3 months

MATERIALS
Bedspread Weight Cotton Thread (size 10):
    Blue - 105 yards
    White - 12 yards
Steel crochet hook, size 7 (1.65 mm) **or** size needed
    for gauge
Sewing needle and thread
Size 4/0 sew-on snaps - 2
$^3/_8$" Buttons - 2

GAUGE: 18 dc = 2"

Gauge Swatch: $1^3/_4$"w x $3^3/_4$"h
Work same as Sole.

SOLE
With Blue, ch 22.

Rnd 1 (Right side)**:** 7 Dc in fourth ch from hook **(3 skipped chs count as first dc)**, dc in each ch across to last ch, 8 dc in last ch; working in free loops of beginning ch *(Fig. 3b, page 2)*, dc in next 17 chs; join with slip st to first dc: 50 dc.

Note: Loop a short piece of thread around any stitch to mark Rnd 1 as **right** side.

Rnd 2: Ch 3 **(counts as first dc, now and throughout)**, dc in same st, 2 dc in each of next 7 dc, dc in next 17 dc, 2 dc in each of next 8 dc, dc in each dc around; join with slip st to first dc: 66 dc.

Rnd 3: Ch 3, dc in same st and in next dc, 2 dc in next dc, (dc in next dc, 2 dc in next dc) 6 times, dc in next 10 dc, place marker around last dc made for st placement, dc in next 8 dc, 2 dc in next dc, (dc in next dc, 2 dc in next dc) 7 times, dc in each dc around; join with slip st to first dc, finish off: 82 dc.

INSTEP
With White, ch 4; join with slip st to form a ring.

Rnd 1 (Right side)**:** Ch 3, 19 dc in ring; join with slip st to first dc: 20 dc.

Rnd 2: Ch 1, sc in same st, ch 3, skip next dc, ★ sc in next dc, ch 3, skip next dc; repeat from ★ around; join with slip st to first sc: 10 ch-3 sps.

Rnd 3: Slip st in first ch-3 sp, ch 1, sc in same sp, (3 dc, ch 1, 3 dc) in next ch-3 sp, ★ sc in next ch-3 sp, (3 dc, ch 1, 3 dc) in next ch-3 sp; repeat from ★ around; join with slip st to first sc, finish off: 35 sts and 5 ch-1 sps.

Rnd 4: With **right** side facing, join Blue with slip st in first dc to left of joining; ch 3, hdc in next dc, sc in next dc and in next ch-1 sp, sc in next dc, hdc in next dc, dc in next dc and in sp **before** next sc *(Fig. 4, page 2)*, dc in next sc and in sp **before** next dc, dc in next dc, hdc in next dc, sc in next dc, ★ 3 sc in next ch-1 sp, sc in next dc, hdc in next dc, dc in next dc and in sp **before** next sc, dc in next sc and in sp **before** next dc, dc in next dc, hdc in next dc, sc in next dc; repeat from ★ once **more**, sc in next ch-1 sp and in next dc, hdc in next dc, dc in next dc, ch 41; leaving remaining sts unworked and being careful not to twist ch, join with slip st to first dc, do **not** finish off: 41 sts.

SIDES
Rnd 1: Ch 3, working in Back Loops Only *(Fig. 1, page 1)*, dc in next 40 sts, dc in each ch around; join with slip st to **both** loops of first dc: 82 dc.

Rnds 2 and 3: Ch 3, dc in both loops of next dc and each dc around; join with slip st to first dc.

Rnd 4: Ch 1, sc in same st and in each dc around; join with slip st to first sc, do **not** finish off.

JOINING
Ch 1; with **wrong** sides of Sides and Sole together, matching first sc on Sides with marked dc on Sole and working through **both** loops of **both** pieces, sc in same st and in each st around; join with slip st to first sc, finish off.

RIBBING
RIGHT BOOTIE
Foundation Rnd: With **right** side facing, toe of Bootie to right and working in free loops of ch on Rnd 4 of Instep, join Blue with slip st in first ch; ch 1, sc in next ch and in each ch across, 2 sc in end of Rnd 4; working in unworked sts on Rnd 3, dc in sp **before** next sc, dc in next sc and in sp **before** next dc, skip next dc, hdc in next dc, sc in next dc, skip next ch-1 sp, sc in next dc, hdc in next dc, skip next dc, dc in sp **before** next sc and in next sc, dc in sp **before** next dc, 2 sc in end of Rnd 4; join with slip st to first sc, finish off: 54 sts.

Row 1: With **right** side facing, skip first 7 sc on Foundation Row and join Blue with slip st in next sc; ch 5, sc in second ch from hook and in next 3 chs (flap made), sc in same st as joining and in each st across; do **not** join: 58 sc.

Row 2: Ch 11, turn; sc in second ch from hook and in each ch across, slip st in first 2 sc on Row 1: 10 sc.

Row 3: Turn; skip first 2 slip sts, sc in Back Loop Only of next 10 sc.

Row 4: Ch 1, turn; sc in Back Loop Only of next 10 sc, slip st in **both** loops of next 2 sc on Row 1.

Rows 5-59: Repeat Rows 3 and 4, 27 times; then repeat Row 3 once **more**.

Finish off.

LEFT BOOTIE

Foundation Row: Work same as Right Bootie: 54 sts.

Row 1: With Blue, ch 4; with **right** side facing, skip first 32 sc on Foundation Rnd and slip st in next sc; ch 1, sc in next sc and in each st across, sc in same st as joining and in next 4 chs (flap made); do **not** join: 58 sc.

Rows 2-59: Complete same as Right Bootie.

Finish off.

Sew snap and button to Ribbing, having flap to inside.

---

4. STARS & STRIPES

Finished Size: 0-3 months

MATERIALS
Bedspread Weight Cotton Thread (size 10):
    Red - 65 yards
    Blue - 12 yards
    White - 12 yards
Steel crochet hook, size 7 (1.65 mm) **or** size needed
    for gauge
Sewing needle and thread
Star buttons - 2

GAUGE: 18 dc = 2"

Gauge Swatch: 1³/₄"w x 3³/₄"h
Work same as Sole.

INSTEP
With Blue, ch 13.

Row 1 (Right side)**:** Dc in fourth ch from hook **(3 skipped chs count as first dc, now and throughout)** and in each ch across to last ch, 8 dc in last ch; working in free loops of beginning ch *(Fig. 3b, page 2)*, dc in next 10 chs: 28 dc.

Note: Loop a short piece of thread around any stitch to mark Row 1 as **right** side.

Row 2: Ch 3 **(counts as first dc, now and throughout)**, turn; dc in next 9 dc, 2 dc in each of next 8 dc, dc in last 10 dc: 36 dc.

Row 3: Ch 3, turn; dc in next 9 dc, 2 dc in next dc, (dc in next dc, 2 dc in next dc) 7 times, dc in last 11 dc; finish off: 44 dc.

STRAP
Rnd 1: With **right** side of Instep facing and working in Back Loops Only *(Fig. 1, page 1)*, join Red with slip st in first dc; ch 1, sc in same st and in each dc around, ch 38; being careful not to twist ch, join with slip st to **both** loops of first sc.

Rnd 2: Ch 1, do **not** turn; sc in both loops of same st and each sc and each ch around; join with slip st to first sc, finish off: 82 sc.

SIDES
Row 1: With **right** side facing, join White with slip st in first sc; ch 1, sc in same st and in next 43 sc, leave remaining sc unworked: 44 sc.

Row 2: Ch 1, turn; sc in each sc across; finish off.

Row 3: With **right** side facing, join Red with slip st in first sc; ch 1, sc in same st and in each sc across.

Row 4: Ch 1, turn; sc in each sc across; finish off.

Row 5: With **right** side facing, join White with slip st in first sc; ch 1, sc in same st and in each sc across.

Row 6: Ch 1, turn; sc in each sc across; finish off.

SOLE (Make 2)
With Red, ch 22.

Rnd 1 (Right side)**:** 7 Dc in fourth ch from hook, dc in each ch across to last ch, 8 dc in last ch; working in free loops of beginning ch, dc in next 17 chs; join with slip st to first dc: 50 dc.

Note: Mark Rnd 1 as **right** side.

Rnd 2: Ch 3, dc in same st, 2 dc in each of next 7 dc, dc in next 17 dc, 2 dc in each of next 8 dc, dc in each dc around; join with slip st to first dc: 66 dc.

Rnd 3: Ch 3, dc in same st and in next dc, 2 dc in next dc, (dc in next dc, 2 dc in next dc) 6 times, dc in next 18 dc, 2 dc in next dc, (dc in next dc, 2 dc in next dc) 7 times, dc in each dc around; join with slip st to first dc, finish off: 82 dc.

Repeat for second Sole; at end of Rnd 3, do **not** finish off.

JOINING
Ch 1; with **wrong** sides of Soles together, matching sts and working through **both** loops of **both** pieces, sc in first 31 dc; with **wrong** side of Sides and **right** side of top Sole together, working through **both** loops of sts on all 3 pieces, sc in next 44 sts; working through **both** loops of **both** Soles, sc in last 7 sc; join with slip st to first sc, finish off.

EDGING
TOP
With **right** side facing and working in free loops of beginning ch on Strap, join Red with slip st in same st as joining; ch 1, sc in each ch around, work 15 sc evenly spaced across Instep; join with slip st to first sc, finish off.

BOTTOM
With **right** side facing and toe of Bootie to left, join Red with slip st in same sc as Joining of all 3 pieces; ch 1, work 6 sc evenly spaced across end of rows on Sides, sc in each sc across Strap, work 6 sc evenly spaced across end of rows on Sides, slip st in same sc as Joining; finish off.

Using photo as a guide for placement, sew button to top of Instep.

5. HAPPY HOLIDAYS

Finished Size: 0-3 months

MATERIALS
Bedspread Weight Cotton Thread (size 10):
  Red - 70 yards
  White - 50 yards
Steel crochet hook, size 7 (1.65 mm) **or** size needed
  for gauge
Tapestry needle
Green and Yellow embroidery floss
Sewing needle and thread
Size 4/0 sew-on snaps - 2
Christmas buttons - 2

GAUGE: 18 dc = 2"

Gauge Swatch: 1³/₄"w x 3³/₄"h
Work same as Sole.

STITCH GUIDE

ADDING ON DOUBLE CROCHETS
When instructed to add on dc at the end of a row, YO,
insert hook into base of last dc *(Fig. 6)*, YO and pull
up a loop (3 loops on hook), YO and draw through
one loop on hook, (YO and draw through 2 loops on
hook) twice. Repeat as many times as instructed.

Fig. 6

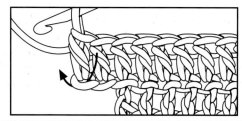

SOLE
With Red, ch 22.

Rnd 1 (Right side)**:** 7 Dc in fourth ch from hook
**(3 skipped chs count as first dc, now and
throughout)**, dc in each ch across to last ch, 8 dc in last
ch; working in free loops of beginning ch *(Fig. 3b,
page 2)*, dc in next 17 chs; join with slip st to first dc:
50 dc.

Note: Loop a short piece of thread around any stitch to
mark Rnd 1 as **right** side.

Rnd 2: Ch 3 **(counts as first dc, now and
throughout)**, dc in same st, 2 dc in each of next 7 dc,
dc in next 17 dc, 2 dc in each of next 8 dc, dc in each
dc around; join with slip st to first dc: 66 dc.

Rnd 3: Ch 3, dc in same st and in next dc, 2 dc in next
dc, (dc in next dc, 2 dc in next dc) 6 times, dc in next
10 dc, place marker around last dc made for st
placement, dc in next 8 dc, 2 dc in next dc, (dc in next
dc, 2 dc in next dc) 7 times, dc in each dc around; join
with slip st to first dc, finish off: 82 dc.

INSTEP
With Red, ch 13.

Row 1 (Right side)**:** Dc in fourth ch from hook and in
next 8 chs, 8 dc in last ch; working in free loops of
beginning ch, dc in next 10 chs: 28 dc.

Note: Mark Row 1 as **right** side.

Row 2: Ch 3, turn; dc in next 9 dc, 2 dc in each of
next 8 dc, dc in last 10 dc: 36 dc.

Row 3: Ch 3, turn; dc in next 9 dc, 2 dc in next dc, (dc
in next dc, 2 dc in next dc) 7 times, dc in last 11 dc;
finish off: 44 dc.

SIDES
Rnd 1: With **right** side facing, join White with slip st in
last dc made on Row 3 of Instep; ch 38, being careful
not to twist ch, slip st in first dc on Row 3; ch 3, dc in
next dc and in each dc and each ch around; join with
slip st to first dc: 82 dc.

Rnds 2-6: Ch 1, sc in same st and in each st around;
join with slip st to first sc.

Rnd 7: Ch 3, dc in next sc and in each sc around; join
with slip st to first dc, finish off.

JOINING
With **wrong** sides of Sole and Sides together, matching
marked dc on Sole and first sc on Sides, and working
through **both** loops of **both** pieces, join Red with slip st
in first st; ch 1, sc in same st and in each st around; join
with slip st to first sc, finish off.

CUFF
RIGHT BOOTIE
Row 1: With **right** side facing and working in free loops
of ch, join Red with slip st in first ch; ch 3, dc in each ch
across to Instep, 2 dc in end of each of next 6 rows, dc
in top of last dc on Instep, add on 3 dc (flap made)
(Fig. 6): 54 dc.

Row 2: Ch 1, turn; sc in each dc across.

Row 3: Ch 3, turn; dc in next dc and in each dc across.

Rows 4-6: Repeat Rows 2 and 3 once, then repeat
Row 2 once **more**; at end of Row 6, finish off.

Edging: With **right** side facing, join White with slip st at
base of Cuff; ch 1, sc evenly around entire Cuff and flap
working 3 sc in each corner; finish off.

LEFT BOOTIE
Row 1: With Red, ch 5, dc in fourth ch from hook and
in next ch (flap made); with **right** side facing, dc in top of
first dc on Instep, 2 dc in end of each of next 6 rows;
working in free loops of ch, dc in each ch across; do **not**
join: 54 dc.

Rows 2-6: Work same as Right Bootie.

Edging: With **right** side facing, join White with slip st at
base of flap; ch 1, sc evenly around entire flap and Cuff
working 3 sc in each corner; finish off.

7

FINISHING

Thread tapestry needle with 6 strands of Green embroidery floss. Following Chart and using photo as a guide for placement, add back stitch trees around Sides (Rnds 3-5) *(Fig. 5, page 2)*, and work cross stitch trunks on Rnd 6.

Thread tapestry needle with 6 strands of Yellow embroidery floss. Add cross stitch star to top of each tree (on Rnd 2).

Sew button and snap to Cuff, having flap to outside.

CHART

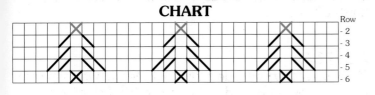

6. BUNNY HOPPERS

Finished Size: 0-3 months

MATERIALS

Bedspread Weight Cotton Thread (size 10):
  Pink - 120 yards
  White - 16 yards
Steel crochet hook, size 7 (1.65 mm) **or** size needed for gauge
Small safety pin
Tapestry needle
Pink embroidery floss
Sewing needle and thread
Bunny buttons - 2
$^1/_8$"w Ribbon - 1 yard

GAUGE: 18 dc = 2"

Gauge Swatch: $1^3/_4$"w x $3^3/_4$"h
Work same as Sole.

STITCH GUIDE

SMALL POPCORN
Ch 3, 4 dc in same st, drop loop from hook, insert hook in top of beginning ch-3, hook dropped loop and pull through **(closing st made)**.

BEGINNING LARGE POPCORN
Ch 3, 6 dc in same st, drop look from hook, insert hook in top of beginning ch-3, hook dropped loop and pull through **(closing st made)**.

LARGE POPCORN
7 Dc in same st, drop loop from hook, insert hook in first dc of 7-dc group, hook dropped loop and pull through **(closing st made)**.

WORKING AROUND A CHAIN
Work **around** chs indicated, inserting hook in direction of arrow *(Fig. 7)*.

Fig. 7

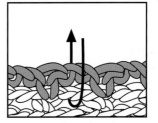

SOLE

With Pink, ch 22.

Rnd 1 (Right side)**:** 7 Dc in fourth ch from hook **(3 skipped chs count as first dc, now and throughout)**, dc in each ch across to last ch, 8 dc in last ch; working in free loops of beginning ch *(Fig. 3b, page 2)*, dc in next 17 chs; join with slip st to first dc: 50 dc.

Note: Loop a short piece of thread around any stitch to mark Rnd 1 as **right** side.

Rnd 2: Ch 3 **(counts as first dc, now and throughout)**, dc in same st, 2 dc in each of next 7 dc, dc in next 17 dc, 2 dc in each of next 8 dc, dc in each dc around; join with slip st to first dc: 66 dc.

Rnd 3: Ch 3, dc in same st and in next dc, 2 dc in next dc, (dc in next dc, 2 dc in next dc) 6 times, dc in next 18 dc, 2 dc in next dc, (dc in next dc, 2 dc in next dc) 7 times, dc in each dc around; join with slip st to first dc: 82 dc.

Rnd 4: Ch 1, sc in same st and in each dc around to last 6 dc, place marker around last sc made for st placement, sc in last 6 dc; join with slip st to first sc; finish off.

Continued on page 9.

INSTEP

With Pink, ch 11.

Row 1 (Right side): Dc in fourth ch from hook and in each ch across to last ch, 8 dc in last ch; working in free loops of beginning ch, dc in next 8 chs: 24 dc.

Note: Mark Row 1 as **right** side.

Row 2: Ch 4 **(counts as first dc plus ch 1, now and throughout)**, turn; skip next dc, dc in next dc, (ch 1, skip next dc, dc in next dc) 3 times, (ch 1, dc in next dc) 7 times, (ch 1, skip next dc, dc in next dc) across: 15 ch-1 sps.

Row 3: Ch 3, turn; (dc in next ch-1 sp and in next dc) 3 times, (2 dc in next ch-1 sp, dc in next dc) 4 times, 3 dc in next ch-1 sp, dc in next dc, (2 dc in next ch-1 sp, dc in next dc) 4 times, (dc in next ch-1 sp and in next dc) 3 times, ch 41; being careful not to twist ch, join with slip st to first dc: 41 dc.

Begin working in rnds.

Rnd 1: Ch 3, working in Back Loops Only *(Fig. 1, page 1)*, dc in next dc and in each dc and each ch around; join with slip st to first dc, place loop from hook onto safety pin to keep piece from unraveling while working Rabbits: 82 dc.

RABBITS
HEADS

First Rabbit: With **right** side facing and toe of Bootie to left, join White with slip st in second dc to **right** of joining;　ch 4, slip st in second ch from hook and in next 2 chs, slip st in same dc as joining　, work Small Popcorn, ch 3, slip st in same dc as joining, repeat from　to　once; finish off.

Rabbits 2-5: With **right** side facing, skip next 10 dc from previous Rabbit and join White with slip st in next dc;　ch 4, slip st in second ch from hook and in next 2 chs, slip st in same dc as joining　, work Small Popcorn, ch 3, slip st in same st as joining, repeat from　to　once; finish off.

BODIES

With **right** side facing, join White with slip st in first dc of Small Popcorn on first Rabbit; work Beginning Large Popcorn, (ch 10 **loosely**, work Large Popcorn in first dc of next Small Popcorn) 4 times; finish off.

SIDES

Rnd 1: With **right** side facing, place loop from safety pin onto hook; ch 3, dc in next 8 dc, keeping Rabbit Heads to front, slip st in closing st of next Small Popcorn, (dc in next 10 dc, slip st in closing st of next Small Popcorn) 3 times, dc in each dc around to last Small Popcorn, slip st in closing st of last Small Popcorn, dc in last dc; join with slip st to first dc: 77 dc and 5 slip sts.

Rnd 2: Ch 3, dc in next 8 dc, keeping Rabbit Body to front and ch-10 to back, slip st in closing st of next Large Popcorn, (dc in next 10 dc, slip st in closing st of next Large Popcorn) 3 times, dc in each dc around to Beginning Large Popcorn, slip st in closing st of Beginning Large Popcorn, dc in last dc; join with slip st to first dc.

Rnd 3: Ch 3, working **around** ch-10 between Rabbit Bodies *(Fig. 7, page 8)*, dc in next 8 dc and in next slip st, (dc in next 10 dc and in next slip st) 3 times, dc in each dc around to last 2 sts, dc in next slip st and in last dc; join with slip st to first dc: 82 dc.

Rnd 4: Ch 1, sc in same st and in each dc around; join with slip st to first sc, do **not** finish off.

JOINING

Ch 1; with **wrong** sides of Sides and Sole together, matching first sc on Sides with marked sc on Sole, and working through **both** loops of **both** pieces, sc in same st and in each sc around; join with slip st to first sc, finish off.

CUFF

Rnd 1: With **right** side facing, toe of Bootie to right, and working in free loops of ch, join Pink with slip st in first ch; ch 1, sc in each ch around, work 13 sc evenly spaced across end of rows on Instep; join with slip st to first sc: 54 sc.

Rnd 2: Ch 4, skip next sc, ★ dc in next sc, ch 1, skip next sc; repeat from ★ around; join with slip st to first dc: 27 ch-1 sps.

Rnd 3: Slip st in first ch-1 sp, ch 3, dc in same sp, 2 dc in each ch-1 sp around; join with slip st to first dc: 54 dc.

Rnd 4: Ch 1, sc in same st and in each dc around; join with slip st to first sc.

Rnds 5-7: Repeat Rnds 2-4.

Finish off.

FINISHING

Using photo as a guide for placement:
Tack Ears in place.
Using 3 strands of embroidery floss, add inner ear.
Using two strands of White crochet thread, add French knot tail to each Rabbit *(Fig. 8)*.
Sew button to Instep.
Weave an 18" length of ribbon through sps on Rnd 2 of Cuff.

Fig. 8

12

8

7

11a

7. ROSEBUD BOOTIES

Finished Size: 0-3 months

MATERIALS
Bedspread Weight Cotton Thread (size 10):
    White - 105 yards
    Green - 5 yards
    Pink - 4 yards
Steel crochet hook, size 7 (1.65 mm) **or** size needed
    for gauge
Tapestry needle
$1/8$"w Ribbon - 1 yard

GAUGE: 18 dc = 2"

Gauge Swatch: $1^3/_4$"w x $3^3/_4$"h
Work same as Sole.

SOLE
With White, ch 22.

Rnd 1 (Right side)**:** 7 Dc in fourth ch from hook **(3 skipped chs count as first dc, now and throughout)**, dc in each ch across to last ch, 8 dc in last ch; working in free loops of beginning ch **(Fig. 3b, page 2)**, dc in next 17 chs; join with slip st to first dc: 50 dc.

Note: Loop a short piece of thread around any stitch to mark Rnd 1 as **right** side.

Rnd 2: Ch 3 **(counts as first dc, now and throughout)**, dc in same st, 2 dc in each of next 7 dc, dc in next 17 dc, 2 dc in each of next 8 dc, dc in each dc around; join with slip st to first dc: 66 dc.

Rnd 3: Ch 3, dc in same st and in next dc, 2 dc in next dc, (dc in next dc, 2 dc in next dc) 6 times, dc in next 18 dc, 2 dc in next dc, (dc in next dc, 2 dc in next dc) 7 times, dc in next 10 dc, place marker around last dc made for st placement, dc in each dc around; join with slip st to first dc, finish off: 82 dc.

INSTEP
With White, ch 11.

Row 1 (Right side)**:** Dc in fourth ch from hook and in each ch across to last ch, 8 dc in last ch; working in free loops of beginning ch, dc in next 8 chs: 24 dc.

Note: Mark Row 1 as **right** side.

Row 2: Ch 4 **(counts as first dc plus ch 1, now and throughout)**, turn; skip next dc, dc in next dc, (ch 1, skip next dc, dc in next dc) 3 times, (ch 1, dc in next dc) 7 times, (ch 1, skip next dc, dc in next dc) across: 15 ch-1 sps.

Row 3: Ch 3, turn; (dc in next ch-1 sp and in next dc) 3 times, (2 dc in next ch-1 sp, dc in next dc) 4 times, 3 dc in next ch-1 sp, dc in next dc, (2 dc in next ch-1 sp, dc in next dc) 4 times, (dc in next ch-1 sp and in next dc) 3 times, ch 41; being careful not to twist ch, join with slip st to first dc, do **not** finish off: 41 dc.

SIDES
Rnd 1 (Right side)**:** Ch 1, sc in same st and in each dc and each ch around; join with slip st to first sc: 82 sc.

Rnd 2: Ch 3, dc in next sc and in each sc around; join with slip st to first dc.

Rnd 3: Ch 1, sc in same st and in each dc around; join with slip st to first sc.

Rnd 4: Ch 4, skip next sc, ★ dc in next sc, ch 1, skip next sc; repeat from ★ around; join with slip st to first dc: 41 ch-1 sps.

Rnd 5: Ch 1, sc in same st and in each ch-1 sp and each dc around; join with slip st to first sc: 82 sc.

Rnd 6: Ch 3, dc in next sc and in each sc around; join with slip st to first dc, do **not** finish off.

JOINING
Ch 1; with **wrong** sides of Sides and Sole together, matching first dc on Sides with marked dc on Sole, and working through **inside** loops of **both** pieces, sc in same st and in each st around; join with slip st to first sc, finish off.

CUFF
Rnd 1: With **right** side facing, toe of Bootie to right and working in free loops of ch, join White with slip st in first ch; ch 1, sc in each ch around, work 13 sc evenly spaced across end of rows on Instep; join with slip st to first sc: 54 sc.

Rnd 2 (Eyelet rnd)**:** Ch 4, skip next sc, ★ dc in next sc, ch 1, skip next sc; repeat from ★ around; join with slip st to first dc: 27 ch-1 sps.

Rnd 3: Slip st in first ch-1 sp, ch 1, sc in same sp, (ch 5, sc in next ch-1 sp) around, ch 2, dc in first sc to form last ch-5 sp.

Rnd 4: Ch 1, sc in last ch-5 sp made, (ch 5, sc in next ch-5 sp) around, ch 2, dc in first sc to form last ch-5 sp.

Rnd 5: Ch 1, sc in last ch-5 sp made, ch 2, (sc in next ch-5 sp, ch 2) around; join with slip st to first sc.

Rnd 6: Slip st in first ch-2 sp, ch 1, (sc, ch 3, sc) in same sp and in each ch-2 sp around; join with slip st to first sc, finish off.

ROSEBUD
With Pink, ch 20; (sc, ch 3, sc) in second ch from hook, ★ skip next ch, (sc, ch 3, sc) in next ch; repeat from ★ across; finish off leaving a long end for sewing.

Beginning with first sc, roll piece tightly and sew through all thicknesses at base of Rosebud to secure; do **not** cut end.

11

LEAF (Make 3)

With Green, ch 7; dc in fourth ch from hook and in next ch, hdc in next ch, 3 sc in last ch; working in free loops of beginning ch, hdc in next ch, dc in next ch, (dc, ch 3, slip st) in same ch as first dc; finish off leaving a long end for sewing.

FINISHING

Using photo as a guide for placement, sew Rosebud and Leaves to Instep.

Weave an 18" length of ribbon through Eyelet rnd.

---

8. LITTLE LADY SLIPPERS

Finished Size: 0-3 months

MATERIALS
Bedspread Weight Cotton Thread (size 10): 70 yards
Steel crochet hook, size 7 (1.65 mm) **or** size needed for gauge
Sewing needle and thread
Ribbon roses - 2
1/8"w Ribbon - 1 yard

GAUGE: 18 dc = 2"

Gauge Swatch: 1³/₄"w x 3³/₄"h
Work same as Sole.

STITCH GUIDE

> **SINGLE CROCHET DECREASE**
> *(abbreviated sc decrease)*
> Pull up a loop in next 2 dc, YO and draw through all 3 loops on hook **(counts as one sc)**.
>
> **DOUBLE CROCHET DECREASE**
> *(abbreviated dc decrease)* (uses next 2 dc)
> ★ YO, insert hook in **next** dc, YO and pull up a loop, YO and draw through 2 loops on hook; repeat from ★ once **more**, YO and draw through all 3 loops on hook **(counts as one dc)**.

SOLE
Ch 22.

Rnd 1 (Right side)**:** 7 Dc in fourth ch from hook **(3 skipped chs count as first dc)**, dc in each ch across to last ch, 8 dc in last ch; working in free loops of beginning ch **(Fig. 3b, page 2)**, dc in next 17 chs; join with slip st to first dc: 50 dc.

Note: Loop a short piece of thread around any stitch to mark Rnd 1 as **right** side.

Rnd 2: Ch 3 **(counts as first dc, now and throughout)**, dc in same st, 2 dc in each of next 7 dc, dc in next 17 dc, 2 dc in each of next 8 dc, dc in each dc around; join with slip st to first dc: 66 dc.

Rnd 3: Ch 3, dc in same st and in next dc, 2 dc in next dc, (dc in next dc, 2 dc in next dc) 6 times, dc in next 18 dc, 2 dc in next dc, (dc in next dc, 2 dc in next dc) 7 times, dc in next 6 dc, place marker around last dc made for st placement, dc in last 12 dc; join with slip st to first dc, finish off: 82 dc.

SIDES
Rnd 1 (Right side)**:** With **right** side facing and working in Back Loops Only **(Fig. 1, page 1)**, join thread with slip st in marked dc; ch 1, sc in same st and in each dc around; join with slip st to **both** loops of first sc.

Rnd 2: Ch 3, dc in both loops of next sc and each sc around; join with slip st to first dc.

Rnd 3: Ch 3, dc in next 8 dc, dc decrease 16 times, dc in next dc and in each dc around; join with slip st to first dc: 66 dc.

Rnd 4: Ch 3, dc in next 8 dc, dc decrease 8 times, dc in next dc and in each dc around; join with slip st to first dc: 58 dc.

Rnd 5: Ch 1, sc in same st and in next 8 dc, sc decrease 4 times, sc in next dc and in each dc around; join with slip st to first sc, do **not** finish off: 54 sc.

CUFF
Rnd 1 (Eyelet rnd)**:** Ch 13, being careful not to twist ch, skip next 22 sc, slip st in next sc, ch 4 **(counts as first dc plus ch 1)**, skip next sc, (dc in next sc, ch 1, skip next sc) 15 times, dc in same st as joining, ch 1, skip next ch, (dc in next ch, ch 1, skip next ch) 6 times; join with slip st to first dc: 23 ch-1 sps.

Rnd 2: Slip st in first ch-1 sp, ch 1, sc in same sp, ch 2, (sc in next ch-1 sp, ch 2) around; join with slip st to first sc.

Rnd 3: (Slip st, ch 2, hdc) in next ch-2 sp and in each ch-2 sp around; join with slip st to first slip st, finish off.

EDGING
With **right** side facing, join thread with slip st in first sc skipped on Rnd 5 of Sides; ch 2, hdc in same st, [skip next 2 sc, (slip st, ch 2, hdc) in next sc] 3 times, [skip next sc, (slip st, ch 2, hdc) in next sc] twice, skip next 2 sc, [(slip st, ch 2, hdc) in next sc, skip next 2 sc] twice, slip st in same sc as ch-13; 2 sc in each sp across ch-13; join with slip st to first slip st, finish off.

FINISHING
Using photo as a guide for placement, sew ribbon rose to Instep.

Weave an 18" length of ribbon through Eyelet rnd.

9. BE MINE

Finished Size: 0-3 months

MATERIALS
Bedspread Weight Cotton Thread (size 10):
    White - 85 yards
    Pink - 7 yards
Steel crochet hook, size 7 (1.65 mm) **or** size needed
    for gauge
1/8"w Ribbon - 1 yard

GAUGE: 18 dc = 2"

Gauge Swatch: 1 3/4"w x 3 3/4"h
Work same as Sole.

STITCH GUIDE

> **TREBLE CROCHET** (abbreviated tr)
> YO twice, insert hook in sc indicated, YO and pull
> up a loop (4 loops on hook), (YO and draw through
> 2 loops on hook) 3 times.

SOLE
With White, ch 22.

Rnd 1 (Right side): 7 Dc in fourth ch from hook
(3 skipped chs count as first dc), dc in each ch
across to last ch, 8 dc in last ch; working in free loops of
beginning ch **(Fig. 3b, page 2)**, dc in next 17 chs; join
with slip st to first dc: 50 dc.

Note: Loop a short piece of thread around any stitch to
mark Rnd 1 as **right** side.

Rnd 2: Ch 3 **(counts as first dc, now and
throughout)**, dc in same st, 2 dc in each of next 7 dc,
dc in next 17 dc, 2 dc in each of next 8 dc, dc in each
dc around; join with slip st to first dc: 66 dc.

Rnd 3: Ch 3, dc in same st and in next dc, 2 dc in next
dc, (dc in next dc, 2 dc in next dc) 6 times, dc in next
18 dc, 2 dc in next dc, (dc in next dc, 2 dc in next dc) 7
times, dc in each dc around; join with slip st to first dc,
finish off: 82 dc.

INSTEP
With Pink, ch 6; join with slip st to form a ring.

Rnd 1 (Right side): Ch 1, 14 sc in ring; join with slip st
to first sc: 14 sc.

Note: Mark Rnd 1 as **right** side.

Rnd 2: Ch 4, 2 tr in each of next 2 sc, 2 dc in each of
next 2 sc, 2 hdc in each of next 2 sc, ch 1, tr in next sc,
ch 1, 2 hdc in each of next 2 sc, 2 dc in each of next
2 sc, 2 tr in each of next 2 sc, ch 4; join with slip st to
slip st at base of beginning ch-4: 25 sts and 10 chs.

Rnd 3: Ch 1, sc in first 4 chs, working in Back Loops
Only **(Fig. 1, page 1)**, sc in next 12 sts, sc in next ch,
3 sc in next tr, sc in next ch, sc in next 12 sts, sc in last
4 chs; join with slip st to first sc, finish off: 37 sc.

Rnd 4: With **right** side facing and working in both
loops, skip first 4 sc and join White with slip st in next
sc; ch 1, sc in same st, ch 3, skip next sc, (sc in next sc,
ch 3, skip next sc) 6 times, (sc, ch 3) twice in next sc,
skip next sc, (sc in next sc, ch 3, skip next sc) 6 times,
place marker around last ch-3 made for st placement, (sc
in next sc, ch 3, skip next sc) twice, pull up a loop in
each of next 2 sc, YO and draw through all 3 loops on
hook, ch 3, skip next sc, sc in next sc, ch 3, skip next sc;
join with slip st to first sc, do **not** finish off: 19 ch-3 sps.

SIDES
Rnd 1: Slip st in first ch-3 sp, ch 39, being careful not
to twist ch, slip st in marked ch-3 sp; ch 1, **turn**; sc in
each ch across, 3 sc in each of next 3 ch-3 sps, 3 hdc in
next ch-3 sp, 3 dc in each of next 3 ch-3 sps, sc in next
ch-3 sp, 3 dc in each of next 3 ch-3 sps, 3 hdc in next
ch-3 sp, 3 sc in each of next 3 ch-3 sps; join with slip st
to first sc: 82 sts.

Rnd 2: Ch 4 **(counts as first dc plus ch 1, now
and throughout)**, skip next st, ★ dc in next st, ch 1,
skip next st; repeat from ★ around; join with slip st to
first dc: 41 ch-1 sps.

Rnd 3: Slip st in first ch-1 sp, ch 1, sc in same sp, ch 3,
(sc in next ch-1 sp, ch 3) around; join with slip st to first
sc.

Rnd 4: Slip st in first ch-3 sp, ch 4, (dc in next ch-3 sp,
ch 1) around; join with slip st to first dc.

Rnd 5: Slip st in first ch-1 sp, ch 1, sc in same sp, ch 2,
(sc in next ch-1 sp, ch 2) around; join with slip st to first
sc, do **not** finish off.

JOINING
Ch 1; with **wrong** sides of Sides and Sole together,
matching 2 dc on Sole with each ch-2 sp on Sides, and
working through **both** pieces, 2 sc in each ch-2 sp
around; join with slip st to first sc, finish off.

CUFF
Rnd 1: With **right** side facing, toe of Bootie to right
and working in free loops of ch, join White with slip st in
first ch; ch 1, sc in same ch, ch 3, (skip next ch, sc in
next ch, ch 3) across to Instep, sc in first unworked
ch-3 sp on Instep, ch 3, (sc in next ch-3 sp, ch 3) 3
times; join with slip st to first sc: 24 ch-3 sps.

Rnd 2 (Eyelet rnd): Slip st in first ch-3 sp, ch 4, (dc in
next ch-3 sp, ch 1) around; join with slip st to first dc.

Rnd 3: Ch 4, (dc in next dc, ch 1) around; join with
slip st to first dc.

Rnd 4: Slip st in first ch-1 sp, ch 1, sc in same st, ch 3, (sc
in next ch-1 sp, ch 3) around; join with slip st to first sc.

Rnds 5 and 6: Slip st in first ch-3 sp, ch 1, sc in same
sp, ch 3, (sc in next ch-3 sp, ch 3) around; join with
slip st to first sc.

Finish off.

Weave an 18" length of ribbon through Eyelet rnd.

10. LITTLE LOAFERS

Finished Size: 0-3 months

MATERIALS
Bedspread Weight Cotton Thread (size 10):
    Blue - 80 yards
    White - 15 yards
Steel crochet hook, size 7 (1.65 mm) **or** size needed
    for gauge
Sewing needle and thread
³/₈" Buttons - 2
¹/₈"w Ribbon - 1 yard

GAUGE: 18 dc = 2"

Gauge Swatch: 1³/₄"w x 3³/₄"h
Work same as Sole.

STITCH GUIDE

> **SINGLE CROCHET DECREASE**
> *(abbreviated sc decrease)* (uses next 2 sc)
> Pull up a loop in next 2 sc, YO and draw through all
> 3 loops on hook **(counts as one sc)**.
>
> **HALF DOUBLE CROCHET DECREASE**
> *(abbreviated hdc decrease)* (uses next 2 sts)
> ★ YO, insert hook in **next** st, YO and pull up a
> loop; repeat from ★ once **more**, YO and draw
> through all 5 loops on hook **(counts as one hdc)**.

SOLE
With Blue, ch 22.

Rnd 1 (Right side)**:** 7 Dc in fourth ch from hook
(3 skipped chs count as first dc), dc in each ch
across to last ch, 8 dc in last ch; working in free loops of
beginning ch *(Fig. 3b, page 2)*, dc in next 17 chs; join
with slip st to first dc: 50 dc.

Note: Loop a short piece of thread around any stitch to
mark Rnd 1 as **right** side.

Rnd 2: Ch 3, dc in same st, 2 dc in each of next 7 dc,
dc in next 17 dc, 2 dc in each of next 8 dc, dc in each dc
around; join with slip st to top of beginning ch-3: 66 sts.

Rnd 3: Ch 3, dc in same st and in next dc, 2 dc in next
dc, (dc in next dc, 2 dc in next dc) 6 times, dc in next
18 dc, 2 dc in next dc, (dc in next dc, 2 dc in next dc) 7
times, dc in each dc around; join with slip st to top of
beginning ch-3: 82 sts.

Rnd 4: Ch 1, sc in same st and in each dc around; join
with slip st to Back Loop Only of first sc *(Fig. 1,
page 1)*, do **not** finish off.

SIDES
Rnd 1 (Right side)**:** Ch 3, dc in Back Loop Only of next
sc and each sc around; join with slip st to top of
beginning ch-3.

Rnd 2: Ch 3, dc in both loops of next dc and each dc
around; join with slip st to top of beginning ch-3.

Rnd 3: Ch 3, skip next dc, ★ hdc in next dc, ch 1, skip
next dc; repeat from ★ around; join with slip st to second
ch of beginning ch-3: 41 ch-1 sps.

Rnd 4: Slip st in first ch-1 sp, ch 1, 2 sc in same sp and
in each ch-1 sp around; join with slip st to first sc: 82 sc.

Rnd 5: Ch 1, sc in same st and in next 32 sc, place
marker in sc just made for Instep placement, sc in each
sc around; join with slip st to first sc, finish off.

INSTEP
Row 1: With **right** side facing, join Blue with slip st in
Back Loop Only of marked sc, do **not** remove marker;
ch 2 **(counts as first hdc, now and throughout)**,
working in Back Loops Only, hdc in next 9 sc,
hdc decrease, (hdc in next sc, hdc decrease) 7 times, hdc
in next 10 sc, leave remaining 39 sc unworked: 35 hdc.

Row 2: Ch 2, turn; working in Front Loops Only, hdc
in next 9 hdc, hdc decrease 8 times, hdc in last 9 hdc:
27 hdc.

Row 3: Ch 1, turn; working in Back Loops Only, sc in
first 10 hdc, pull up a loop in each of next 7 hdc, YO
and draw through all 8 loops on hook **(counts as one
sc)**, sc in last 10 hdc: 21 sc.

Row 4: Ch 1, turn; working in Front Loops Only, sc in
first 9 sc, pull up a loop in each of next 3 sc, YO and
draw through all 4 loops on hook, sc in last 9 sc; do **not**
finish off.

Joining: Turn, fold Row 4 in half with **right** side
together; matching sts and working in **inside** loops only,
slip st in each st across; finish off.

FLAP
Row 1: With **right** side facing, join Blue with slip st in
marked sc on Sides; ch 1, work 13 sc evenly spaced
across end of rows on Instep.

Row 2 (Right side)**:** Ch 1, turn; sc in Back Loop Only of
each sc across.

Rows 3-7: Ch 1, turn; working in both loops,
sc decrease, sc in each sc across to last 2 sc, sc decrease:
3 sc.

Finish off.

Edging: With **right** side of Flap facing and working in
end of rows, join White with slip st in Row 2; ch 1, sc in
same row and in next 5 rows; working in sts on Row 7,
2 sc in first sc, sc in next sc, 2 sc in last sc, sc in end of
first 6 rows; finish off.

CUFF
Rnd 1: With **right** side facing, join Blue with slip st in
first unworked sc on Sides; ch 3, dc in next sc and in
each sc around to Instep, ch 5, working in free loops of
sc on Row 1 of Flap *(Fig. 3a, page 2)*, skip first 5 sc, sc
in next 3 sc, ch 5, skip last 5 sc; join with slip st to top
of beginning ch-3, do **not** finish off: 42 sts and 10 chs.

Continued on page 15.

14

Rnd 2 (Eyelet rnd)**:** Ch 4 **(counts as first dc plus ch 1)**, skip next dc, ★ dc in next st, ch 1, skip next st; repeat from ★ around; join with slip st to first dc: 26 ch-1 sps.

Rnd 3: Slip st in first ch-1 sp, ch 3, (hdc in next ch-1 sp, ch 1) around; join with slip st to second ch of beginning ch-3, finish off.

Rnd 4: With **right** side facing, join White with slip st in any ch-1 sp; ch 2, hdc in same sp, (slip st, ch 2, hdc) in each sp around; join with slip st to first slip st, finish off.

TRIM

With **right** side and top of Bootie facing, working in free loops on Rnd 4 of Sole, join White with slip st in any st; ch 1, sc in same st and in each st around; join with slip st to first sc, finish off.

Fold Flap over Instep.

Using photo as a guide for placement, sew button to top of Flap sewing through all thicknesses.

Weave an 18" length of ribbon through Eyelet rnd.

11a. GIRL'S SANDALS

Finished Size: 0-3 months

MATERIALS
Bedspread Weight Cotton Thread (size 10):
  White - 45 yards
  Variegated - 40 yards
Steel crochet hook, size 7 (1.65 mm) **or** size needed for gauge
Sewing needle and thread
³/₈" Buttons - 2

GAUGE: 18 dc = 2"

Gauge Swatch: 1³/₄"w x 3³/₄"h
Work same as Sole.

STITCH GUIDE

> **TREBLE CROCHET** *(abbreviated tr)*
> YO twice, insert hook in st indicated, YO and pull up a loop (4 loops on hook), (YO and draw through 2 loops on hook) 3 times.
>
> **BEGINNING DOUBLE DECREASE**
> (uses next 2 sts)
> ★ YO, insert hook in **next** st, YO and pull up a loop, YO and draw through 2 loops on hook; repeat from ★ once **more**, YO and draw through all 3 loops on hook **(counts as one dc).**
>
> **DOUBLE DECREASE** (uses next 3 sts)
> ★ YO, insert hook in **next** st, YO and pull up a loop, YO and draw through 2 loops on hook; repeat from ★ 2 times **more**, YO and draw through all 4 loops on hook **(counts as one dc).**

SOLE (Make 2)
With White, ch 22.

Rnd 1 (Right side)**:** 7 Dc in fourth ch from hook **(3 skipped chs count as first dc)**, dc in each ch across to last ch, 8 dc in last ch; working in free loops of beginning ch *(Fig. 3b, page 2)*, dc in next 17 chs; join with slip st to first dc: 50 dc.

Note: Loop a short piece of thread around any stitch to mark Rnd 1 as **right** side.

Rnd 2: Ch 3 **(counts as first dc, now and throughout)**, dc in same st, 2 dc in each of next 7 dc, dc in next 17 dc, 2 dc in each of next 8 dc, dc in each dc around; join with slip st to first dc: 66 dc.

Rnd 3: Ch 3, dc in same st and in next dc, 2 dc in next dc, (dc in next dc, 2 dc in next dc) 6 times, dc in next 18 dc, 2 dc in next dc, (dc in next dc, 2 dc in next dc) 7 times, dc in each dc around; join with slip st to first dc, finish off: 82 dc.

Repeat for second Sole.

JOINING
Rnd 1: With **wrong** sides of Soles together, matching sts, and working through **both** loops of **both** pieces, join Variegated with slip st in same st as joining; ch 1, sc in same st and in each dc around; join with slip st to Back Loop Only of first sc *(Fig. 1, page 1)*.

Rnd 2: Ch 1, working in Back Loops Only, sc in same sc and in next 38 sc, place marker around last sc made for Strap placement, sc in next 25 sc, place marker around last sc made for Strap placement, sc in next 13 sc, place marker around last sc made for Instep placement, sc in last 5 sc; join with slip st to **both** loops of first sc, finish off.

INSTEP
Row 1: With **right** side facing, join Variegated with slip st in both loops of marked sc for Instep; ch 3, dc in next 11 sc, ch 7, skip next 12 sc, dc in next 12 sc: 24 dc and 7 chs.

Row 2: Ch 1, turn; sc in each dc and in each ch across: 31 sc.

Row 3: Ch 2, turn; work beginning double decrease, work double decrease 3 times, skip next 2 sc, sc in next 3 sc, skip next 2 sc, work double decrease 4 times: 11 sts.

Row 4: Ch 1, turn; sc in each st across.

Row 5: Ch 2, turn; ★ YO, insert hook in **next** st, YO and pull up a loop, YO and draw through 2 loops on hook; repeat from ★ 9 times **more**, YO and draw through all 11 loops on hook, ch 1 to close; finish off: one st.

Toe Edging: With **right** side facing and Toe away from you, join Variegated with slip st in same sc on Rnd 2 of Joining as first dc on Row 1 of Instep; ch 1, work 12 sc evenly spaced across, slip st in same sc on Rnd 2 of Joining as last dc on Row 1 of Instep; finish off.

Instep Edging: With **right** side and Toe facing you, join Variegated with slip st in same marked sc on Rnd 2 of Joining as first dc on Row 1 of Instep; ch 1, work 19 sc evenly spaced across, slip st in same sc on Rnd 2 of Joining as last dc on Row 1 of Instep; finish off.

ANKLE STRAP
RIGHT SANDAL
Right Foundation Row: With **right** side facing, join Variegated with slip st in first marked sc, do **not** remove marker; ch 3, dc in next 4 sc; finish off: 5 dc.

Left Foundation Row: With **right** side facing, join Variegated with slip st in next marked sc, do **not** remove marker; ch 3, dc in next 4 sc; finish off: 5 dc.

Row 1: With Variegated, ch 18; with **wrong** side of Left Foundation Row facing, sc in next 5 dc, ch 20; with **wrong** side of Right Foundation Row facing, sc in next 5 dc: 10 sc.

Row 2: Ch 3, turn; dc in next 4 sc and in each ch and each sc across to last ch, tr in last ch; finish off.

Heel Edging: With **right** side facing, join Variegated with slip st in marked sc for Left Foundation Row; ch 1, work 3 sc across end of rows; working in free loops of ch, sc in each ch across; work 3 sc across end of rows, slip st in same sc on Rnd 2 of Joining as last dc on Right Foundation Row; finish off.

Top Edging: With **right** side facing, join Variegated with slip st in marked sc for Right Foundation Row; ch 1, work 5 sc evenly spaced across end of rows; 3 sc in first dc on Row 2, sc in each dc across, 3 sc in next tr, 2 sc around post of tr (buttonhole loop); working in free loops of beginning ch, 3 sc in first ch, sc in each ch across; work 3 sc across end of rows, slip st in same sc on Rnd 2 of Joining as last dc on Left Foundation Row; finish off.

LEFT SANDAL
Right Foundation Row: With **right** side facing, join Variegated with slip st in first marked sc, do **not** remove marker; ch 3, dc in next 4 sc; finish off: 5 dc.

Left Foundation Row: With **right** side facing, join Variegated with slip st in next marked sc, do **not** remove marker; ch 3, dc in next 4 sc; do **not** finish off: 5 dc.

Row 1: Ch 1, turn; sc in first 5 dc, ch 20; with **wrong** side of Right Foundation Row facing, sc in next 5 dc: 10 sc.

Row 2: Ch 21, turn; dc in fifth ch from hook and in each ch and each sc across; finish off.

Heel Edging: With **right** side facing, join Variegated with slip st in marked sc for Left Foundation Row; ch 1, work 3 sc across end of rows; working in free loops of ch, sc in each ch across; work 3 sc across end of rows, slip st in same sc on Rnd 2 of Joining as last dc on Right Foundation Row; finish off.

Top Edging: With **right** side facing, join Variegated with slip st in marked sc for Right Foundation Row; ch 1, work 3 sc across end of rows, working in free loops of beginning ch, sc in each ch across to ch-4 sp, 7 sc in ch-4 sp (buttonhole loop); sc in each dc across to last dc, 3 sc in last dc; work 5 sc evenly spaced across end of rows, slip st in same sc on Rnd 2 of Joining as last dc on Left Foundation Row; finish off.

Sew button to Ankle Strap.

11b. BOY'S SANDALS

Finished Size: 0-3 months

MATERIALS
Bedspread Weight Cotton Thread (size 10): 85 yards
Steel crochet hook, size 7 (1.65 mm) **or** size needed for gauge
Sewing needle and thread
$5/16$" Buttons - 2

GAUGE: 18 dc = 2"

Gauge Swatch: $1^3/4$"w x $3^3/4$"h
Work same as Sole.

STITCH GUIDE

TREBLE CROCHET (abbreviated tr)
YO twice, insert hook in st indicated, YO and pull up a loop (4 loops on hook), (YO and draw through 2 loops on hook) 3 times.

BEGINNING DOUBLE DECREASE
(uses next 2 sts)
★ YO, insert hook in **next** st, YO and pull up a loop, YO and draw through 2 loops on hook; repeat from ★ once **more**, YO and draw through all 3 loops on hook **(counts as one dc)**.

DOUBLE DECREASE (uses next 3 sts)
★ YO, insert hook in **next** st, YO and pull up a loop, YO and draw through 2 loops on hook; repeat from ★ 2 times **more**, YO and draw through all 4 loops on hook **(counts as one dc)**.

SOLE (Make 2)
Ch 22.

Rnd 1 (Right side)**:** 7 Dc in fourth ch from hook **(3 skipped chs count as first dc)**, dc in each ch across to last ch, 8 dc in last ch; working in free loops of beginning ch **(Fig. 3b, page 2)**, dc in next 17 chs; join with slip st to first dc, do **not** finish off: 50 dc.

Note: Loop a short piece of thread around any stitch to mark Rnd 1 as **right** side.

Continued on page 17.

Rnd 2: Ch 3 (counts as first dc, now and throughout), dc in same st, 2 dc in each of next 7 dc, dc in next 17 dc, 2 dc in each of next 8 dc, dc in each dc around; join with slip st to first dc: 66 dc.

Rnd 3: Ch 3, dc in same st and in next dc, 2 dc in next dc, (dc in next dc, 2 dc in next dc) 6 times, dc in next 18 dc, 2 dc in next dc, (dc in next dc, 2 dc in next dc) 7 times, dc in each dc around; join with slip st to first dc, finish off: 82 dc.

Repeat for second Sole; at end of Rnd 3, do **not** finish off.

JOINING

Rnd 1: Ch 1; with **wrong** sides of Soles together, matching sts, and working through **both** loops of **both** pieces, sc in same st and in each dc around; join with slip st to Back Loop Only of first sc *(Fig. 1, page 1)*.

Rnd 2: Ch 1, working in Back Loops Only, sc in same sc and in next 38 sc, place marker around last sc made for Strap placement, sc in next 25 sc, place marker around last sc made for Strap placement, sc in next 13 sc, place marker around last sc made for Instep placement, sc in last 5 sc; join with slip st to **both** loops of first sc, finish off.

INSTEP

Row 1: With **right** side facing, join thread with slip st in both loops of marked sc for Instep; ch 3, dc in next 11 sc, ch 7, skip next 12 sc, dc in next 12 sc: 24 dc and 7 chs.

Row 2: Ch 1, turn; sc in each dc and in each ch across: 31 sc.

Row 3: Ch 2, turn; work beginning double decrease, work double decrease 3 times, skip next 2 sc, sc in next 3 sc, skip next 2 sc, work double decrease 4 times: 11 sts.

Row 4: Ch 1, turn; sc in each st across.

Row 5: Ch 2, turn; ★ YO, insert hook in **next** st, YO and pull up a loop, YO and draw through 2 loops on hook; repeat from ★ 9 times **more**, YO and draw through all 11 loops on hook, ch 1 to close; finish off: one st.

Toe Edging: With **right** side facing and Toe away from you, join thread with slip st in same sc on Rnd 2 of Joining as first dc on Row 1 of Instep; ch 1, work 12 sc evenly spaced across, slip st in same sc on Rnd 2 of Joining as last dc on Row 1 of Instep; finish off.

Instep Edging: With **right** side and Toe facing you, join thread with slip st in same marked sc on Rnd 2 of Joining as first dc on Row 1 of Instep; ch 1, work 19 sc evenly spaced across, slip st in same sc on Rnd 2 of Joining as last dc on Row 1 of Instep; finish off.

ANKLE STRAP
RIGHT SANDAL

Right Foundation Row: With **right** side facing, join thread with slip st in first marked sc, do **not** remove marker; ch 3, dc in next 4 sc; finish off: 5 dc.

Left Foundation Row: With **right** side facing, join thread with slip st in next marked sc, do **not** remove marker; ch 3, dc in next 4 sc; finish off: 5 dc.

Row 1: Ch 18; with **wrong** side of Left Foundation Row facing, sc in next 5 dc, ch 20; with **wrong** side of Right Foundation Row facing, sc in next 5 dc: 10 sc.

Row 2: Ch 3, turn; dc in next 4 sc and in each ch and each sc across to last ch, tr in last ch; finish off.

Heel Edging: With **right** side facing, join thread with slip st in marked sc for Left Foundation Row; ch 1, work 3 sc across end of rows; working in free loops of ch, sc in each ch across; work 3 sc across end of rows, slip st in same sc on Rnd 2 of Joining as last dc on Right Foundation Row; finish off.

Top Edging: With **right** side facing, join thread with slip st in marked sc for Right Foundation Row; ch 1, work 5 sc evenly spaced across end of rows; 3 sc in first dc on Row 2, sc in each dc across, 3 sc in next tr, 2 sc around post of tr (buttonhole loop); working in free loops of beginning ch, 3 sc in first ch, sc in each ch across; work 3 sc across end of rows, slip st in same sc on Rnd 2 of Joining as last dc on Left Foundation Row; finish off.

LEFT SANDAL

Right Foundation Row: With **right** side facing, join thread with slip st in first marked sc, do **not** remove marker; ch 3, dc in next 4 sc; finish off: 5 dc.

Left Foundation Row: With **right** side facing, join thread with slip st in next marked sc, do **not** remove marker; ch 3, dc in next 4 sc; do **not** finish off: 5 dc.

Row 1: Ch 1, turn; sc in first 5 dc, ch 20; with **wrong** side of Right Foundation Row facing, sc in next 5 dc: 10 sc.

Row 2: Ch 21, turn; dc in fifth ch from hook and in each ch and each sc across; finish off.

Heel Edging: With **right** side facing, join thread with slip st in marked sc for Left Foundation Row; ch 1, work 3 sc across end of rows; working in free loops of ch, sc in each ch across; work 3 sc across end of rows, slip st in same sc on Rnd 2 of Joining as last dc on Right Foundation Row; finish off.

Top Edging: With **right** side facing, join thread with slip st in marked sc for Right Foundation Row; ch 1, work 3 sc across end of rows; working in free loops of beginning ch, sc in each ch across to ch-4 sp, 7 sc in ch-4 sp (buttonhole loop); sc in each dc across to last dc, 3 sc in last dc; work 5 sc evenly spaced across end of rows, slip st in same sc on Rnd 2 of Joining as last dc on Left Foundation Row; finish off.

Sew button to Ankle Strap.